PRAISE FOR LINDS1
WHERE WATER MEETS THE ROCK

John Donne used "metaphysical conceit," the comparison of two extremely different ideas. Lindsey Martin-Bowen revives this form as she sets Greek gods into contemporary places, like Psyche in a Hy-Vee grocery. "Hood Ornament" illustrates her invention: "I'm silver—not gold—/Mercury coasting on/a wind that eclipses roses." Martin-Bowen's wonderful poetry is for book lovers, as she revives the gods, Oliver Twist, and many others in her metafictive dances with words. This book is sheer fun.

—Denise Low
Kansas Poet Laureate 2007–2009
author of *The Turtle's Beating Heart* (U of Nebraska Press 2017)

Where Water Meets the Rock is a returning to the early works of an established poet. I loved Lindsey Martin-Bowen's first three volumes, but I adore this one. It follows on the heels of the developed works by an established artist, treating me to her early poems and the chance to retrace the pathways to an artist's developing maturity. In these poems, Lindsey swings for the fences with wordplay and a keen sense of humor ripe with allusions made new again as they resonate with today's tumble-turvy world. Check out "Re-Reading 'The Second Coming' by W.B. Yeats" to make sense of racially charged confrontations in Ferguson, Missouri. In "Frenzies Rush In," get ready to meet a cadre of characters who reach out from both our literary canon and recent pop culture. Don't be surprised to find Data from *Star Trek* bump up against Oliver Twist and Jack Sprat. Playfulness and unexpected juxtapositions alert us to be ready for anything, because anything can happen. The least expected action can pop open like a Jack-in-the-box surprising us with insight.

—Robert Haynes
Writing Certification Program Director 2005–2015, AZ State University
author of *Grand Unified Theory* (Paladin Contemporaries 2001)

WHERE WATER MEETS THE ROCK

also by Lindsey Martin-Bowen

Poetry

Crossing Kansas with Jim Morrison
(Paladin Contemporaries 2016)

Inside Virgil's Garage
(Chatter House Press 2013)

Standing on the Edge of the World
(Woodley Press 2008)

Second Touch
(Chapbook 1990)

Fiction

Rapture Redux: A Comedy
(Paladin Contemporaries 2014)

Hamburger Haven
(Paladin Contemporaries 2009)

Cicada Grove
(Paladin Contemporaries 1992)

WHERE WATER MEETS THE ROCK

poems by

LINDSEY MARTIN-BOWEN

Lindsey Martin-Bowen

39 WEST
PRESS

39 WEST PRESS
Kansas City, MO
www.39WestPress.com

39 WEST
Ⓟ Ⓡ Ⓔ Ⓢ Ⓢ

First Edition: July 2017

ISBN: 978-1-946358-05-9

Library of Congress Control Number: 2017942503

This book is a work of fiction. Names, characters, places, dates, and incidents are products of the author's imagination, or are used fictitiously, satirically, or as parody. Any resemblance to actual persons, living or dead, business establishments, events, or locales is entirely coincidental.

10 9 8 7 6 5 4 3 2 1

Design, Layout, Edits: j.d.tulloch
Front & Back Cover Photos (Cape Kiwanda Pacific City, OR): j.d.tulloch

39WP-22

*For Tina Hacker, Alarie Tennille, Jeanie Wilson,
and Maryfrances Wagner—four superb women
poets who have encouraged me by both their
words and actions.*

CONTENTS

EROSION

FRENZIES RUSH IN

ON THE SHORE

EROSION

The yew in my yard
grows red berries round and sweet
as last night's kisses.
I worry they may wither
when a scorching summer comes.

—Tanka Yew

Pasiphaë Regrets (Wife of Minos II*)

I'm tied to a bull I cannot marry.
The cost would be too dear:
I'd lose my kingdom,
my distraught children,
who'd inherit my shame,
and my last shard of dignity.

Had the king not been such a skunk,
I wouldn't be in this predicament.
And how I wish now Daëdalus
would have denied my request.
He knew what was best
but feared my revenge.

Today, I stare at the Aegean.
A part of me wants to dive in,
sink to the bottom, a stone, cold
and heartless—an entity alone,
lured by the beauty of a beast
whose white belly undid me.

*The son of Minos I, the King whom the gods named Judge of the underworld.
Minos II was not so honorable. His wife fell in love with the bull because Minos
II was supposed to sacrifice the animal to Poseidon. Instead, he kept the beast for
himself. For revenge, Poseidon made Pasiphaë fall in love with the bull.

Psyche in the Suburbs

Lord, I've got to shop for her again—
such a queen bee she is—always,
me-me-me, that Aphrodite.
So I shove a cart down Hy-Vee aisles,
stop and toss in Pop-Tarts for her grains.
Then wouldn't you know it, I slip
and slam into a display of seeds,

spilling millet, barley, poppy, and rye
on linoleum. I bend to sort them
and thumb through gold skeins
for her silly sewing circle. I tell you,
my mother-in-law leaves me dazed—
I wander around shelves of creams
and aloe lotions that form a maze.

Now, lavender scents fill the air,
sending me to the Aegean Sea.
When I step onto the asphalt,
I remember the bottled water.
I must go back. Without it,
the world will know her face
grows old. And she'll blame me.

Backyard Burial

Something's up.
Two crows hop onto the fence.
They flutter back-feathers
and lift their claws
in a waltz—St. Vitus swooping

along a cliff, his hands linked
to a long line of dancers. I toss the birds
stale cracker crumbs from my pantry.
They cackle.

Then, in the grass, I see the rabbit.
Fresh blood circles its twisted head,
one open eye glazed, like the eyes
at Carthage,
Rome or Troy fallen into ruins—

I'll bury the carcass before the July
sun rots it, before the crows feast.
I break hard dirt under the oak.
I am Antigone, defying
an unfair edict—

the lawnmower, a broken chariot—
a relic marking this grave.
Roosting on a phone line,
the crows laugh like pagan gods.

VC in the City

Henry's so sick of the jungle,
he can't lift his head.
And Lord, he hears another
chopper beating
ahead. Almost breathless,
he waits—
with fists poised to hit
any rustle in leaves,
any sound not his.

They hiss like locusts
in maples, crawl across gravel,
stumble around bushes at the edge
of a road. They duck behind
deli counters, squint
under fluorescents, cop
some stash, squeeze triggers,
and point them at his neck.
But he can't catch them.

Two shots whiz by his head,
but no one else hears them.
No one but Henry sees
the tracers, watches soldiers
scramble, smells the catgut
in their paths. And he still
tastes sulfate as he twitches
in a corner in the white
room down the hall.

Since You Left

to my mother

My plants refuse to speak to me.
I drag around a silent household,
listen for your words in each room,
and shuffle past an empty table.
There, morning sunlight glints
off that spot where, yesterday,
you left your glasses.

Today, smells of dying roses
linger, and light spreads across
the wall, unlike last night,
when candlelight carved shadows
deep as your eyes while you exhaled
one last breath. Your moans of pain
became too intense for words.

But now I miss those groans
when I hear nothing—no
sounds, except the thuds
of the water heater
and the thunder
of the furnace
firing its last.

About Mangan's Sister*

with apologies to James Joyce

Under streetlights, a girl without a name
waits for you. She fingers a railing
then twists a silver bracelet.

Dim light from gas lamps halos the curve
of her neck, and you become a ship at sea,
circling constellations and a weary moon.

Above harpoons, you watch sails billow
in wind, filling like the hem of her petticoat.
She talks about an Eastern bazaar,

where jars guard shop stalls, and cheap
cut-glass looks like rubies, sapphires,
or diamonds so real,

they reflect moonlight off the waves
until it wanes into the dull
luster of love's embers.

*A character in James Joyce's "Araby," a short story in the collection, *Dubliners*, 1914. (First USA publication: B.W. Huelsch, 1916.)

Racing the Rain Home

They're always a problem:
these slick highways.
Vapors rise so quickly:
steam trapped
inside glass—
I feel like Sylvia Plath
when the bell jar dropped.

The fog rolls on and on,
more like some lion's claws
than any kitten's feet.
It fills my windshield,
and I shimmy on asphalt
over a bridge. I slide
then skid and skid.

Still, I steer the car,
pull ahead of the rain.
But I'm unsure
if I'm winning this race
or if I'm caught
in the eye
of a hurricane.

When Hat Dated a Beret

The problem was, she couldn't get used
to his lisp and the smell of cigarettes
on her brim after she two-stepped
with him in the days of Coco Chanel,
when hats paraded along the Seine.

After thirty years, she tried again.
By then, he'd managed to stay in closets
or go for walks to the market—
away from bars and cigarette
smoke. But in that nasal lisp,

he told her it wouldn't work—
she needed a new look: no ostrich feathers
and wide brims with black gauzy streamers.
In fact, he said, few women don hats.
Long ago, Chanel closed her shop.

So, she left him there, drinking beer
and staring at the Seine. Sometimes,
when a stream of black felt flies by,
she pictures him—a black mustache
frowning at a barge pulling from the shore.

Hood Ornament

I'm silver—not gold—
Mercury coasting on
a wind that eclipses roses
woven into a trellis
in a yard edging
the back road where
we fly over ruts
and treads slap asphalt.
My heart beats faster
with each tire's rotation
as I watch my life dash
by in double-time.

O such a ride it is—till I turn
to wave and fall face-first:
a wheel runs over
one of my legs.
It's often like this—
that backward glance—
reflection of a past,
a last chance we
cannot change,
no matter how fast
we accelerate
to obliterate the pain.

After Reading Milosz*

We sing about oaks, a bumblebee flitting
from bush to bush, and a birdbath
reflecting a yellow sky growing gray.

Here, in our neighborhood's momentous shape,
a dog growls, a cat hisses and hunches its back,
and rain thuds against the asphalt.

It's like this: even if the massacres I've seen
appear solely on small screens, their stench fills
my nostrils while I limp down this empty street.

*Cheslaw Milosz's "The Poor Poet." *Selected Poems Revisited*. The Ecco Press.
1973.

Diamonds in the Sidewalk

At first, they look like slivers
of glass—glimmering specs
of broken goblets.

I try to step around them,
then see they're inside the concrete
forming a tiara around my feet.

Once, I held fistfuls of diamonds—
Daddy bought a spread in South Hampton.
But no more. The money's gone.

It left in the Crash
and took the house,
car, and Daddy's job at the classy
Hy-Cee Glass Company.

Like a girl playing hopscotch,
I maneuver around
the diamond-
studded squares

into the grassy easement.
I no longer care
and trudge uphill
to the dollar store.

Brooklyn Avenue

The girl with brown braids
waves from a window
at the fire-truck, its siren
pulsing as it skids on asphalt
past a fat man in a hammock.
The truck swerves around
an opossum with teeth
from some ancient
archaeology and rolls
down the street to the brown-
stone on the corner,
where last winter,
an elderly woman collapsed,
dropped a basket
of red berries in the snow,
and hit that special place
in the heart so hard
it stopped beating.

It's like that—these
sudden endings—
when faith falls
like a sparrow
with an injured wing
to clay earth.
The heart stops,
pulls out.
Done.

Whiteout

It's empty here,
some ghost town
wrapped in ice.
Everything's white,
a wedding gone awry,
a veil smothering
a bride, this slick street.
We lose our direction.

I try to remember
the trail to the yellow steps
on a cabin we painted
years ago, its potbelly stove
now cold as lights
flashing ahead.
Another car blocks us.
There's no shoulder to pull onto.

We can't go on.

A Softer Parade

after "Forest," the painting by Äsa Antalffy Eriksson

O child of Hawthorne,
must you step again
into black woods,
where gremlins and ogres
could rip open your skull
and twist your brain
into a thousand knots?
You walk in wonder
on dew-covered grass.

Its sweet smell lures you
into black—far away
from this suburb.
Squirming like toads,
clouds of gold and a feather
fight your movements
like Don Quixote and Sancho
battling windmills
that care little for chivalry.

You run from gold clouds
and feathers. A strange wind
hits your back and spurs
you deeper into pines
and aspens. Trees cluster
like a coven of witches
bent over a fiery pot.
Charcoal smells draw
your step into their dance.

Periwinkle Park Armageddon

A ponderosa spreads along the edge
of Periwinkle Park. It's green—
green as Iraq scenes
shot at night in war zones.
We camp for the day, pretend
we're outdoorsmen—sit in vortex
under pines that smell
like bleached logpoles.

A fly circles: its buzzing
interrupts the creek's
high-pitched refrain.
The tiny beast reminds us
war remains everywhere—
how even in this place,
some small beast keeps
me from letting go.

You squint and unfold
a topographical map,
search another route
into pines—far from the city
that squelched your dreams.
Clouds roil into battalions—
they cover the skies.
Armageddon.

Mainly willows line the creek.
In the field, one small aspen
intertwines with pines
aligning like soldiers.
We share a can of kippers,
chase it with cheese,
pack into the truck,
and wait for rain.

The Ghost of Rappaccini's Daughter

A PBS history about poison reports that doctors once used poisons as medicine—often to counteract each other.

Beatrice,* Rappaccini's daughter,
haunts me. Shimmering across my carpet,
she bends over a lily and woos it
with gardenia smells. Then she tells me
she didn't plan to break a heart:
her poison-breath was meant to heal.

Rich as a Tuscan sunset, her voice
infected Guasconti when she agreed
to nurse a shrub back to life.
He didn't understand that plant
was sister to the scientist's daughter
with her green eyes.

She still lives in love's shadow,
she says, and walks in a dimension
Guasconti* can't enter,
no matter how he tries. And
now, she drifts to my backyard
and plucks petals in the dead night.

*Two characters in Nathaniel Hawthorne's short story, "Rappaccini's Daughter."

To Phil Miller*: 2011

You claim you're a ghost,
purse your lips to kiss the wind,
then spew words that rub
our skin like spider webs.
Tonight, your image lingers in layers—
your gossamer ghosts appear,
one tied to an old house
with trembling cross-beams,
maybe the three-story Victorian
where you lived north of here.
And one haunts a street corner
where George Grand leaned
against a lamp post. One hangs out
at Salvation Army thrift stores
where you bought an ashtray or two.
Another hovers outside
a bar's steamy window,
smells damp beer, peers in,
and searches for a face you once knew.
Even if you gave up that funny life
twenty-five years ago
and became kinder to dogs,
cats, and even pigeons,
you still weren't sure if you'd paved
your road to Hell or Heaven.

Yet, on nights like this, when winds
growl in your raspy voice,
I see you up there,
grinning.

*Poet and teacher Phil Miller taught writing and literature at Kansas City, Kansas
Community College for more than 25 years. He contributed extensively to the
Kansas City literary scene, where he started *The Same* literary magazine, gave
poetry workshops and readings, and began the Riverfront Reading Series. He
wore out at age 67.

Wandering Around
Ulysses' Plight

I'm tired, friend, of wandering the docks
and navigating whirlpools and rock.
Smells of fish, coral, and algae won't leave

my nostrils. They follow me in markets,
where I inhale cinnamon, garlic and chili scents—
odors sweeter than any song from a siren.

But here, the dank alleys run narrower than galleys
and darker than a cove in an abandoned inlet.
Creatures like Scylla and Charybdis hover,

make me want to disappear. Despite the pain
in these bowed legs, I must return to waves.
Rocking the deck back and forth, they lull me to sleep.

Your Last Christmas
for my father

Under holly boughs and smells
of evergreen, you sit in an old,
decrepit chair and warn us
you're on your way out.
The image behind your words
becomes another play.
You're John Wayne,
and I'm the extra, a receptacle
for this monologue,

this wagon train rolling west
beyond a sun that's left its glory—
Custer's golden plume of curls—
on a desert trail
where eagles fly backwards
and the air's too thin for mortals,
or, at least, for us flatlanders
who sit along the river
when the fishing's good.

I pray this is just another role:
a man growing old, moving west
toward that eternal precipice.
So I change the subject
to Christmas stockings,
mistletoe left hanging,
smells of myrrh and mincemeat,
a chill in the air
I can't shake.

Cutting Sharply as Saki

Madame Butterfly's retort

Cutting sharply as a Samurai sword,
your words slice my silk kimono
and shear this silver cloth
into a strip that lies like an obi*
across the floor. And those words
pricking my skin remain
after my mosaic heart
shatters into shards,
spilling blood,
sweet as iris scents,
onto a bamboo mat.
The stains remind me
of the day our worlds
separated us, leaving
our lives bitter
as the Saki lingering
on our tongues.

*The sash on a kimono.

Your Last Two Days
to Mother

Late afternoon light filters
through thin Venetian blinds
in this pale room at Liberty
Hospital. Alcohol smells
and other disinfectants
put me on edge. Then I see
your face, ashen again.

Your eyes look clear. You appear
to see me, yet your cries come
from a creature in a trap.
Your shrill howls—the wolf-woman
La Loba's*—don't rebuild your
shin bone. Those howls aren't you—
quiet as a trickling creek—

they're the sound of wind raging.
"You'll have to wear a peg leg,"
I say. "You're a pirate now."
You smile. Your eyes glimmer.
You laugh. Then, an eerie howl
follows. I call La Loba
to resurrect you from pain.

*According to Southwest legends (from various tribes and Mexican cultures),
La Loba (The Wolf Woman) works with angels to gather bones of humans and
wolves. They resurrect their skeletons so the deceased live again.

Roxanne*

It wasn't him, really.
Even if he was pretty,
I fell in love with the wind
wafting lily scents
across the terrace
and up the balcony
on a night when the moon's
an orange floating
on the Mediterranean—
or a pomegranate like one
Cyrano buys me in the market
on days when we talk of love.

I fell for his words—smooth
as dove wings. Cyrano's words
are sugar kisses, too. But his nose
keeps him untouchable. I can't see
behind his grotesque mask—
who can, really? Who sees
beyond the skin, beyond flesh
easily punctured by a knife,
a sword, or even a pin? It bleeds,
yet I still can't see within,
where muscles twitch
like insects about to take flight.

*The heroine in Edmond Rostand's 1897 play *Cyrano de Bergerac.*

Green Light Equinox

Among exhaust fumes, again, I wait.
Like Jay Gatsby squinting across the lake,
I ache for that green go-ahead.

A man in the next lane doesn't seem to care.
He lifts hands high and opens his mouth
as if singing an aria in an opera.

At the corner, a mother pushes a stroller
with a set of twins wearing sky blue hats.
Their giggles and light-weight jackets

show Spring inches in. Smells of lilac
and honeysuckle have hit our suburb.
Iris scents should follow soon.

Storm Season

Now upside down,
the iron chairs
look like Muslims
kneeling in prayer.

We bring in Mother's
yellow cushions to stop
the stench of mold
in this spot where moss

routs garden stones.
Sweet lily smells grow
stronger as petals wither
from hail and intense wind,

and oak limbs bow,
laden with the last rain.
They'll drop lower when
the one blows in today.

My Bones are Glass

with apologies to Mark Strand

My bones are glass.
I move through each day
hearing the same tune
with the same lack of grace.

My bones are glass.
They do not play a sweet melody
but clack in cacophonies
of icicles cracking in wind.

My bones are glass.
They tremble when I inch across
white-coated fields under a cold moon
that signals this strange season.

At Odd Fellows Home Cemetery

Under overcast skies, she waits
at a window in late October,
when a leaf's green is short-lived.
Although it clings to an oak,
it senses the lack of sap flowing
through its veins will force it
to freefall into a downward spiral
and land with its cousins
in a pile on the lawn.

But she isn't thinking of that leaf
or any leaves. She waits
for the call coming soon—
that call igniting the surreal
world of his absence—a world
without smells of his Bay Rum
aftershave, without his touch
and his off-beat gait she'll miss
even more than his kisses.

Messages from My Shower

for Jeanette Powers

Overnight, they appear—almost invisible—
watery hieroglyphics running in rivulets
through steam creeping across glass.
My bones cling to my skin when I try
to decipher these arcane messages.
Then, a voice like pipes hissing
sends me to a sea in Galilee, silver
as the handhold I grab.

"I am Jephthah's daughter," it sings.
"My only sin is greeting Father
when he returns from battle.
I dance and play a tambourine.
But he vowed to sacrifice
the first one he sees.
That person is me.
So I ask two months to mourn
my virginity: a life without issue,
a woman failed."

Later, I read Israelite women still trek
a pilgrimage to mourn her
four days each year.*

I wonder where her bones lie
and why she had to die.

*See *Judges 11: 30-40*.

Re-Reading "The Second Coming" by W.B Yeats

after Ferguson, Missouri

No one listens anymore. No one works
in tandem. No horses pull this cart.
Now trembling, it falls apart.

The center hub's blown, exploded.
Rioting in city squares—rioting along beaches:
is this anarchy—or something more?

The blood of victims rushes onto shores.
Innocents no more, their lungs fill
till they can't speak—can't breathe.

Their passions now senseless, uneasy—
bringing the strange revelation:
the Second Coming lies on the horizon.

It's the day, it's the day—
O yes, it's the holy day—
it's the Day of the Dead.

A wide-winged beast rises above—
eyes black and gleaming, onyx
glistening through bone.

Oh Momma, Momma,
come back, come back
again. This world's too cold.

No lion-bodied beast slouches
toward Bethlehem. It's a creature
with a jackal's head, a jackal's soul.

FRENZIES RUSH IN

The poet's eye in
a fine frenzy rolling, doth
glance from heaven to
earth ... gives to airy nothing
a local habitation ...

—William Shakespeare
(*A Midsummer Night's Dream*)

Economics

Jack Sprat could eat no fat,
so Julio offered him a pickle.
But Jack didn't want that
and swallowed a Big Mac
from a microwave fiber. Supply-
demand, neither could understand,
and meanwhile, the orange juice
grew warmer as it waited
for a Little Mick. A Japanese
passion fruit flew in from Oahu,
rolled in chocolate, and hopped
a ship to the Apple. There,
stocks skyrocketed until
they bottomed
on the line and landed
with Jack and Julio
in an ice cream parlor.

Oliver Twisted

O, what a morning it was—
when two salamanders took off
for London after Mr. Bumble
bloomed roses in Mrs. Squire's
heart. And Edward the Monk
with the map on his face disgraced
Nancy, whom Bill Sykes left
in a bloody heap on her floor.
Meanwhile, Fagan was hanged
in blood-stained silk from Selfridges's
bargain basement, while Ezekiel
cawed, "Nevermore." Then Rose blew
from the web onto Edward Monk's
head when he sailed to the India
holdings. Waving Ta-Ta, the Artful
Dodger strutted along, while Bill's
pit-bull snapped at his heels.

Head Trip

Data left the starship's trek and rescued
Julio from a wreck to help him drive a bus
of Decisions to the college Strategic
meetings. Audrey the Iguana blocked
them because her car broke a gasket
and she needed a ride to the Five & Dime
for a head of cheese to drop in her basket.
"Times awastin," Poppa Decision said,
and he dreaded arriving late at the campus,
where a ruckus exploded in the lot
each morning at nine. So Audrey hopped in
without bringing her kin, her bookish Philippine
cousins who wore Levi jeans and paraded
around the breakfast nook. But before Audrey left,
the iguana kin stacked her car on blocks
and told her to look the other way. Instead,
Audrey gazed into the rear view mirror
where everything appears in reverse.
What's worse, Data hit the accelerator too hard,
and they took off, plopped on the campus lot,
where they disembarked in grasslands
and danced with dandelions forming
a ring around the asphalt canyon.

Regrets Redux

Julio and Isabel skipped school
and decided to plant a garden of regrets,
which the Brits call rue, that grew
in the Italian Alps. They took out a loan
from Jack, whom they'd regret paying back,
when Julio slipped on a slice of cheese
from Monterey, after the festival jazzed it
up with jalapeños. So they phoned Lagrimas
the tall Iguana, a PT in a hacienda
not far from the Vatican border.
Lagrimas stretched Julio's back
till he was over the attack of muscular
anarchy. Then she gave in to drinking
Julio's gin but replaced it with a plastic
Bullwinkle statue. Like a spoiled brat,
Isabel grabbed that statue to join the gnome
in the garden. Before the massage was done,
two nuns arrived with Audrey the Willowy,
who'd spent the night with Richard
before Liz bonked her on the crown
with an empty bottle of Jim Beam.
Then everyone jumped into the pickup
and raced full-throttle to the cottage
on the edge of the foothills. There,
they finally grew a garden of rue,
and now, they sing the Blues
about regrets even still.

Anna Iguanina

Blame the trains—coupling, uncoupling—
clangs banged through Anna's brains—
till she grew insane and ran from Alexéi
(also Karénin) to Count Alexéi (also Vronsky)
and back again because she didn't want
to leave Sergéi (also Alexéich, also Seryózha,
also Kútik) behind. Her head pounded
through pages and pages, and all of these
Russians pondered and wandered
back and forth from St. Petersburg
to Moscow so Alexéi (also Karénin)
could beat his fist on the pow-wow
table. But no one was ready to revolt
yet, so they took another vote. And
only Levin (also Dmitrich, also Kóstya)
thought to till soil and plant wheat
after he left his sweaty feet at the office.
Then the trains railed back onto the scene,
leaving Anna in a lean and mean position.
And at the end, no yeast was left, so all
of them relied on Levin (also Dmitrich,
also Kóstya) to make the crops rise.

Frazzled

Julio wanted mashed potatoes,
so he drove to the kitchen in his beat-up,
red Ford pickup. Whizzing out of the lot,
he spun gravel, and two bald-headed cops
chased him to San Jose. There, they picked up
an armadillo for speeding and let Julio off
with a warning. So he tried not to get caught
in another newspaper scam when he slammed
down his brakes at a truck-stop. He picked up
José, and they sped away to search for Audrey
the Iguana with huge green eyes. Audrey's land-
lady claimed that the Iguana moved away
to the West Coast where she lived
under a highway ramp near dessert dunes.
So Julio and José took another day to stop
for more gas, and then they headed West,
still looking for pudding they could spoon
on the way. When they arrived at 2:45 (AM),
they double-parked the truck at a B & B.
No one was home, so they left alone
and still search the West Coast highways
for Audrey the Iguana today.

Waking Up in the Men's Dorm

Bonita had nowhere to sleep because she lost
her daddy's Jeep in the last revolution.
So she ran to Julio who had connections
in the local pet store, where an iguana
named Nancy worked for seeds and small
change. Nancy gave Julio a lead on a guy
who posted a sign for a roommate
at the center of town. Julio tossed these crumbs
to Bonita, who knew that again and again,
when she dug up dirt, she caught her fingers
in the cash register. So she shrugged and slid
into a stall, then out the door, and ran into
Jimmy the Wrestler. Jimmy slapped cash
down her back, and she used that as a deposit
on a new hacienda. But as it turned out,
the Realtor doubted her clout with the priest
on the corner. So Bonita ducked out
and found a place with Ralph, a student
at the campus for runaway hounds.
This worked until classes resumed
and the dorm-master threw Bonita
out the window. She went back to Jimmy
who wrestled the Realtor and bought
the hacienda on the hill. She lives there still
and bills the dorm-master for headache pills.

When the Cheetos Come Home from College

They've grown a bit rounder—
orange bellies drooping
over their sides—evidence
of the Freshman 15. Too many
restaurant scenes reveal
that tall tale is true. But
they'll eat celery all summer,
they say, to look good in plays
and TV commercials.

They tripped over Aristotle,
and Oedipus made them weep.
So they yak about changing majors
from theatre to movies—
especially those made for TV.
I tell them don't worry:
their talents lie in legends
and folklore, but they
don't listen to me.

I mention Rappaccini's
daughter—how her beauty
deceived the wisest ever.
They shrug then quiver.
This fall, they'll return
to where they learned
the lesson: applause
sounds merely like rain
clouds bumping together.

Fruit Salad

Julio brings
a ripe pineapple.
I worry that a worm
will gnaw through the fruit's
thick husk and bite into sweet,
yellow meat before
Julio can eat it.
     He must know
a slice of pineapple
sweetens a piece of cholla,
even when someone sprinkles
lemon on it—or even
if a star falls from the sky
and chars it,
     the fruit
will stay sweet,
like the sparkle of a girl
dressed with bows
in her hair for her first
formal dance when she's
so young, she still wears
     burlap pants
to jump into a car
as if she were riding
a horse into a barn
after a rough day
of chasing cows
across the plains.

Doldrums

Tied to a bull that drug her
across the prairie, Bonita fell
under the spell of gardenia smells,
though sniffing them made her weary.
So she rolled a tumbleweed for cash
to find Julio on I-70 because he
gave her great deals on old Chevys.
Meanwhile, she fell in with Cedar
and Joan, two chimps from the Valley
who liked to get stoned and eat
mashed potatoes raw with no gravy.
Soon, Bonita left the chimps
for Sloppy Joes, and she bought
a Julio Chevy. Then, she zoomed
East, bought a spread colored red
in the Shenandoah Valley,
and won't go home again.

Doldrums II

O what a squall it is
that swirls us out to sea where Julio
sails in circles while he searches
for the biggest chunk of cheese.
Instead, he finds a Blue Moon—
maybe two—that he follows
over the edge of the world, at least
as far as the horizon leads,
glimmering with that twilight burst
before it's too bright to hide
in the ocean's shadows. And now,
smells of spring swell across Julio's
deck before he swabs it. Then he turns
astern and rams into Eddy the Worm
who's been sailing all day in a closet.
So we leap into a lifeboat and hope
it floats all the way to the office,
after the eighty days of rain
that pounded the frame
and pushed us to dock it.

Still Riding on the Storm

after "Forest," the painting by Äsa Antalffy Eriksson

O what a squall it is—twirling
us out to sea, away from woods,
where Bonita steps through a threshold
and looks for the PJs she lost last week
when she swam under a windmill
until storm clouds roiled and shooed
her inside. There, she spotted a light
so bright, it dropped her into a garden
of regrets. And yet, she still steps
under that doorway every night
to find a way to play with the feather
that forever hovers in her brain. It watches
every movement she makes and reports
each one to the IRA.

Chopped Liver

Julio unrolled his lariat and rode
with drovers while he looked for a cover
to his lap-top TV. And back at the ranch,
Bonita baked a batch of chopped liver
cookies for tonight's Scene. But she stopped
to give her iguana, Nancy, more dancing
lessons. So they cha-cha-cha-ed to the ha-hahs
and stepped into a tango. Meanwhile, Julio
lost his saddle when his horse Sancho lost
the poncho and reared. Along came Bonita
and Nancy, still dancing, which set Sancho
to prancing, so Julio had to chase the horse.
They formed a fine chorus line on the way
to the sun dance at the Gummy Bear breast-
implant factory. Fortunately, the sun
arrived with a hangover at five, smelling
of endive, before the dance was done. So,
they had time to run back to the ranch
and grab the cookies, now for fun.

Split Seconds

Julio tripped over Aristotle because the voices
inside his head led him to toddle to the Raven
and Reader's World, where he sold his book
on macaroni and cheese. Meanwhile,
Ignacio loaded his holster with a paint gun
to have fun at this year's office picnic,
and he waited for Julio by the school garden.
Once Julio arrived, Ignacio stepped inside
the truck, sprayed Julio, who ducked,
and the paint hit a cop in the yard. Of course,
the cop burned red. Then, he pulled out a guitar
and banged it on Ignacio's head. Ignacio
swooned, then ran out but started to pout
while he headed toward the park
where the picnic already ran full-force.
The cop gave chase because he couldn't erase
the red spot on his forehead. Julio followed
them both and hoped he could share some toast
to end the ensuing dispute. Then, Bonita appeared
with her cookies again and waved them at the cop
who stopped for a bite. So, Ignacio escaped
but then met his fate against a paint gun larger
than Chicago. More paint is forecast tomorrow.

Fox Soup

O they hunted so long
that Jane and Liz, Mr. Darcy,
and of course, Mr. Bingley
came along to that grassy space
behind the rose bushes in the front
lawn, where they'll corner the fox
who's been darting left and right,
fighting for his life in this wilderness
called England. But this remains
a pastoral spot, with poplars and oaks
across the lot, far away from London's
Baker Street, long before Sherlock
and John will meet and even longer
before anyone will conspire to erect
the V&A, where Albert and Victoria
rest today, not all that long
after they filled their bellies
with soup made from a fox.

Midnight Train to Paris

It was one of those nights when Isabel
caught her feet at every corner.
So she slipped into a fluffy pink robe
and wandered through *Le Louvre*
and down *l'avenue des Champs-Elysées*
in search of a polyester ferret.
The rodent led her through narrow
paths in underground sewers
with rats and Left Bank detours
all for another ball of cheese.
Then, she sneezed and fell
into *le Quartier Latin*,
where she break-danced
with Johnny the Fiend,
and *Le Moulin Rouge* painter
chased her sweetly. Still,
she ran away to *la tour Eiffel*
and floated over
l'Arc de Triomphe
before she met a gnome
and called it a day at a dark café,
where she met two penguins
named Ray, before hopping
the last train home.

Silent Canopy

in memory of James Tate (December 8, 1943-July 8, 2015)

Under Caribbean skies, a penguin leads his brood
through tall grasses where cockatiels fly and alight
on branches. The arctic birds dart around snakes

and perform poisonous dances and gymnastics
in jagged steps, toes turning inward, whirling
away from vipers until everyone keels over in a sweat.

Most of the penguins don't dig this hot aquatic scene
with thick palms instead of evergreens under skies
flat as blue paint inside a Victorian canopy for a royal

wedding. And smells of poi and hot spices don't do
their bills justice. They prefer salmon from icy seas,
where they swim and dive deep—far from a glowering sun.

Tonight, they'll try not to stink when they soak their feet
in Epsom-salt water, sip a pear drink, and seek out a sailor
to help them find a ball of cheese, the perfect ball of Cheese.

Whirling Dervishes (of random thoughts)

"Some people never go crazy. What boring lives they must lead."
—*Charles Bukowski*

1

St. Francis d'Assisi rode a horse
draped in zebra skins,
a Medieval camouflage
that he thought made him
invisible to opposing warriors.
When I wear my long jumper—
a camouflage—designed to hide
soldiers in foliage or jungle,
I become invisible, too.

2

According to the Catechism,
Jesus was fully God and fully human.
He was especially a human
when he lugged that cross
on his striped back to Golgotha.
There, he left His earth suit
and morphed into pure Divinity—
not the candy, you silly,
but God almighty.

3

Like graffiti on a subway wall,
the ghost of Rappaccini's daughter
haunts me with gardenia smells
and confides her poison breath's
meant to heal. Her lilacs bloomed
today, and this year, they're huge
and smell like chocolate. And look:
the two toadstools down the street
still don't know what's happening.

To Catch Leviathan

Try hooking his lip,
wrapping a noose
around his thick neck
or piercing a spike
into his fierce jaw.

Harpoon his hide, strip it
down to his two layers
of armor with rows
of shields sealed
together.

Avoid his red eyes
shooting lasers
and flames of lightning
coming from
his tongue. Duck
the steam from his nostrils
or prepare to run.

But to trap Leviathan,
track him to
Baton Rouge, Louisiana,
Orlando, Florida,
Falcon Heights, Minnesota,
Overland Park, Kansas,
or anywhere
in Afghanistan.

ON THE SHORE

Silver sand glistens
into diamonds on the shore,
where the water meets
the rock and sleeps for a while
but will rise in fury soon.

—Shoreline Tanka

The Land of Sky Blue Waters
with apologies to James Wright

Forget about the bear paddling
a canoe through neon waves
in this dark bar at the edge of Troost.
A couple huddles in a corner.
Maybe half-drunk, she rests her head
on his shoulder. He kisses her crown
but eyes her breasts.
    I try to ignore those two
so I can tell you about a lake,
the sounds of tom-toms,
water rushing over a cliff,
and twilight shadows filling the sky,
about a place far from plastic cups,
cell phones, and freeways.
    I want to lie in a hammock there,
hide out from this bar,
where I serve rounds
of gin for men, sweaty
and stinking of tar. I want
to lie under a pine, watch
chicken hawks glide
    and squawk at each other.
They fly from their roosts
and soar. Here, waves
keep turning against themselves.
They form a maze
of muddy water: a creek
running dark green, brown, gray.

Twelve and a Half Ways of Looking at a Penguin

1
Near our snow condos,
penguins slide across ice.
No ostrich plumes: these birds
wear sleek, Edwardian suits.

2
I have always walked like a penguin.
In fact, I was born a penguin long ago
in the days when the ice caps were intact.

3
I slipped into church under knotted skies.
There, the gray day plummeted to black.

4
A man and a woman laugh
at penguin prostitution:
the birds must trade sex
for rocks to build nests.

5
I herringboned up hills
and slid on snowfields.
I pecked through tundra
to unearth pebbles—
and often came up empty.

6
Snow clings to branches
and creates an enchanted
silhouette against a gray
horizon. A penguin strolls
along the coast, searching
for her mate.

7

Dr. Fiona Hunter says penguins
stick with the same mates.
But she adds, "Stones are valuable
currency" for them. That
urgency creates reckless hens.

8

Such a day it was—a day
when everything went asunder:
penguins thundered
and cracked the ice
when a sea lion
raped a penguin hen.
But some of the birds didn't care.

9

Take that penguin over there
leaning against a snow-wall.
He stares into space
then waddles to a pool
of balloons rising.

10

You grumble about Christmas
and gatherings—
ignore these birds
sliding by us now—ignore
the calls from family.

11

Your words fall
like frogs from your mouth,
and I say the world will end
soon for these penguins
skidding into the blue.

12
Today, these gregarious birds
waddle into politics.
I'd figured they'd march for ecology,
but no—the feathered creatures
fight for civil rights.

12 ½
I watch a penguin pile stones.
She stops and looks into my eyes.
We do not speak but know.

KC Sky Stations

New Yorker R.M. Fischer created
these stations that watch the city
from far above the streets.
Even if they look like Easter
cakes, they're diligent as legions
guarding a fortress. With gold,
green, and red confections,
these four sky stations flash
lights that take away breath.
They sit atop Bartle Hall,
where vendors and buyers
cluster for conventions
amid coffee and bakery scents.
Few glance up at these guards
high above shoppers
whose lines of vision
focus straight ahead.

Carriage Ride in the Country Club Plaza

The horse canters through
this City of Fountains—
not Rome, not Paris.
This one's the miniature twin
of Seville, Spain. Clay-tile roofs
glisten around a cupola,
and we shudder when a light wind
rolls over our skin, bringing dew
to the backs of our hands.
In an August that feels like autumn,
the light has switched to the silver
glare of shorter days. I flinch
when you squeeze one of my wrists.

The Eyes of Spring

for Rook

The Eyes of Spring watch
red streaks glint off window panes,
and white sheets shimmer on clotheslines.
They spot dandelions edging sidewalks
in Loose Park and follow flights of martins
replacing the crows. In their dance,
the birds whirl, then stop, and fashion a nest
in the bough of an oak. The Eyes of Spring
watch eggs hatch and feathers spring to life.

But the Eyes of Summer lie:
they watch sunlight glistening on white
sand beaches and reflecting off waves.
Then, their sights move inland again
and trace trails of albino squirrels
who leap through peach trees
exploding with fruit from ripe twigs.
They pretend the season will not end.

Vegetable Linguistics

1
Some sprout in earth—dirt,
rich mulch, where molecules
are born, split and fuse into more
cells, then sweet potatoes, carrots,
beets, and rutabagas—roots—
vegetable limbs sinking into blackness,
growing deep, building skin to protect
soft meat from animals and elements.

2
Some blossom—broccoli, cauliflower—
miniature coiffures of granny hair—
and shimmer with dew early during
June and July when morning
glories bloom and climb gates. These
veggies stay awake, feel wind against
their heads, wait for the perfect
hour before they lie in beds.

3
Others are towers—monuments
of phallic energy: asparagus
stems stretch toward the sun,
artichokes spit spiky leaves
at the moon, and celery stalks
grow ridges for strength.
And can we name sugar cane
among these solid shoots?

4
And then come the fungi:
mushrooms bloom in wet
places, show button faces
in spaces where many
dare not step.
Amanita muscaria—
no, not yet.

Two Mothers with Kids in Winchell's
for Aaron

1

One woman lugs a black-haired boy on her hip.
She's rosy-cheeked, pregnancy-plump. "Whoa," she quips
when the tyke squirms, grabs flyers from a counter.
The other, blonde in Estee Lauder, orders
doughnuts. Her fuchsia jogs—immaculate, so clean—
no sweat staining armpits, no grass stains on knees,
not like you and me—in ripped, vagabond jeans.

The mothers in Winchell's nod, talk in buzzing hums,
eye their toddlers, who hop, slide on linoleum.
The kids scratch glass, balance on window ledges.
The pregnant one smooths seersucker. "Guys," she says.
"They don't like that here. Come, be quiet. Sit down."
Like seatbelts, her words rein them in. I frown,
wonder how she renders her voice firm but not loud.

2

And I realize I failed at that with you, my son.
My words rang out in shrieks, and the demon
voices from Dad and Mother taunt me still. Mean
as ever, they rage: "Act your age!" and "You're grungy!"
We aren't dysfunctional—our voices are—jets
spitting vapors that blind us, blur our quests.
Now, they whisper, "Failure," as I write at this desk.

Your sister Ki tells me Grandma makes her change
clothes before eating. "Makes me angry because
it's such a hassle to change again," she says.
"Do you feel you're not good enough?" I ask. Then
she frowns. "No. Just angry." She squints and looks wise.
Of course, she's not her mother, I think. "Do I
make you feel not good enough?" She replies, "No."

3

But Aaron, I know you can no more say that
than I can exorcise words or take them back.
I say I'm sorry. You say you understand.
But your low vowel sounds convince me you're a man
drafted into this war of voices, too.
Harsh ones torpedo sly ones. None side with you.
I pray you'll bestow on them a silent truce.

Then, we'll saunter into Winchell's arm-in-arm,
play the mother-and-son routine with aplomb.
No doubt, the Winchell's mothers will be there.
One pats a kid's head. The other fingers the hair.
And that's okay. We won't show stress or chagrin.
You'll joke about craziness, tap my chin.
We'll see those mothers look up, awed, when we breeze in.

Poems Make Strange Pets

One of them rubs against my leg.
Moving back and forth
in an incessant rhythm,
it whines for my attention.
Or maybe it wants cream
or a cookie, something to crush
in its tight little paws.
Busy figuring taxes,
I ignore its pleas, till finally,
it leaps onto one of my shoulders,
digs in its claws,
and we tumble to the floor.
"Stand up and walk," it huffs
and scrambles into the living room,
where it flings itself on a wall.

Missouri Pegasus

J.C. Nichols Fountain, Country Club Plaza (Kansas City, MO)

Humidity forms tears on his wings,
and he's locked in a fountain
where he leads a warrior
in a circle under water
bouquets that tremble
like iridescent glass.

He and the other bronze horses
carry metal warriors
through diamond sprays—
chemical water arcing
over a fountain in this sister
city to Seville, Spain.

While the horses rear,
the warriors lean back.
Their heads almost dropping
into the waves,
they cede any
conquest.

Missouri Pegasus II

J.C. Nichols Fountain, Country Club Plaza (Kansas City, MO)

His nostrils flare, and his eyes
glare at some vision
we can't yet see.
This steed kicks the air
and rears over water
while his warrior rider
swoons with battle fatigue.

Or maybe Missouri's thick air
and fog shoved the soldier
to depths so low, his spirit's
black as that day
in Golgotha when clouds
festered into onyx knots
then roiled into rain.

Still, lights reflect off the hair
of this equestrian—plummeting
like a stone god eternally lost.
Then, sprays of water
pelt him till he's
fragile as a poem
not yet in flight.

Mushroom Park

at 100 degrees Fahrenheit (near Carneiro, KS)

Over our heads, huge rock
buttons balance on stems—
shapes the gods carved for us
to marvel at while we sweat
and trudge through prairie
grass to scale and inspect
these ancient sculptures.

We run fingers over striated layers,
its lines—eons of wind and rain.
We feel the pain of a landscape
overrun with floods, then shrunken
with drought. A chicken hawk
circles above, and we huddle
under these umbrellas of rock.

Perhaps John Brown once stepped
upon this surreal spot. Amelia Earhart
might have watched these rocks
from her plane's open cockpit.
Today, the stone bowls remain
to create shadows that hide us
from traffic rolling over asphalt.

Spring River Swimmers

From the tracks, first we see nothing.
Then, we spot them—
two girls who shake off water
streaming down their yellow-orange suits.
Then, they shiver in the sun.

Walking where the water hits rock,
they play with a paper boat,
watch it whirl in eddies
that suck in the afternoon light,
and they squat beside the rolling river.

Above them, we struggle for footholds
or gravel that slides like coal dust
from this malleable terrain.

We search for their boat, fading now
as fast as our footprints.

The Day Before Summer Solstice

An orange sun
draws out freckles
on my thighs,
forming star maps—
Andromeda, Cepheus,
and Cassiopeia—
winter constellations
at summer's peak.
Orion shoots an arrow
at my navel.
It hits my black
two-piece with coral
and turquoise blooms,
something Mother
might have liked.

After James Dickey's "Cherrylog Road"

O what a day it was
and so sweet when we
pretended to drive
KC streets in a '53 Chevy
that sat tireless on blocks
at the back of your '65 garage.

Like some stock-car racer,
you steered the wheel
to dodge ruts and other
autos in your head. And I
navigated by staring
through the windshield.

No rattlers or king-snakes
nested in that garage,
and it wasn't abandoned
like some car graveyard
with Pierce-Arrows
and rusted farm wagons.

Just the same, we two
were movie stars, waiting
for the change in scenes
when we could rest
another place together—
a spot between clean sheets.

Stuck with a Deck

for Jim Yates

If this were a ship, these planks
would be Bristol*—a crew would swab
them, keep them watertight. No acorns
would lodge between them—no seeds
would sprout into maples. Sailors
worry more about algae and brine.
These planks split and grow gray
aground here, where moss rots wood
unless it's painted and stained.
No time for owners to read in shade
or sit in the sun with lemonade.

Now, cherry trees bloom white,
and the robin nests again
in the front door wreath:
time for deck grief—
even if it doesn't heel,
this deck pirates too much
time to stay shipshape,
unlike a paver patio
requiring a mere tile
replaced once in a while.

*In good order.

"Brown Sugar" in the Suburbs

Strains of the Rolling Stones' hit
waft through Vista del Verde.
Tonight, a cover band plays
on Gomer's patio, where couples
down highballs and beer
and perhaps a steak or chicken
entrée. The smell of fat
burning follows the drumbeats,
and I hike to those rhythms
on my way to the store.

I swivel my hips like I did
when I took Rook
to a Reggae concert
seven years ago. He's 12
now and goes to dances
with friends only. I glance
at the mauve clouds
spread out like toadstools.
They fade with the moon
rising above a gray horizon.

Sheep Creek Bay

Flaming Gorge National Recreation Area, Utah

Like some ancient scene
in an archaeology magazine,
orange-striped cliffs slip into seas
of mineral salts north of the Unitas.

We might have walked here once:
you in beaver pelts, me in cloth
I wove from sheep wool
I'd wound on a rough spindle.

It's like that—this place:
it brings back memories
we may have shared on this shore
where water meets the rock.

Blue Columbine

An oddity in these environs
of hard rock—aspens,
rugged pines that smell

like Christmas—this fragile
flower withstands harsh winds
and snows in late spring.

My daughter picks a columbine
and gives it to her daughter.
She eats it and blooms.

I Want to Hang Upside Down Somewhere

Far away from here, like a bat
in a cave—yet not a vampire's life—
more like lives of puffins or albatrosses
who spend most days at sea,
away from cell phones, traffic, and PCs.

Some early Christians lived in caves
near Caledonia. They carved out rooms
with smooth walls, some for storage, others
for sleeping: homes safe from weather,
Roman soldiers, and other predators.

If blood rushes to my head, it might open
senses to gardenias and lilac smells
instead of the sick sweetness of antifreeze.
There's relief in this escape: to be new
again, a baby reborn, remade.

Sturgeon Moon on August 18, 2016
also "Red Moon"

Such a moon to be named for a fish, red
as salmon leaping streams in the northwest,
where fish still thrive but not like before
conquistadors came and made the landscape
their whore by stealing gold, agate, lapis, turquoise,
and black gold spouting from earth layers eons old.

Tonight, a sturgeon moon shimmers over a black horizon.
Like a fish, it's oblivious to rubies, conquerors, and wars.
Even if it's the god Nanna, it merely reflects light sent its way.

Mary Magdalene's Gospel

The world's a lie,
He says, but I disagree
when sweet pear scents waft
through a window. I wrap
myself in blue silk, feel it slip
across my breasts, and step
on sand that massages my soles.
    Not until branches
slash my back do I believe.
Then, welts form a gnarled,
chokecherry tree twisted
like those words men use
to cast women
as underlings.
    Except Him. He doesn't
spew worn adages about us,
and He claims love rules the flesh.
He talks of new beginnings
and of life that doesn't end.
I spread oil over His feet,
wipe them with my hair,
    and listen to His words
about this prison that wraps us
in shadows. He rattles its bars
till they shatter, breaks a hole
into the skies, takes my hands,
and pulls me through—
me, a woman scorned.

River Rafting

White water rushes in Colorado rivers,
even in the quiet *Cache la Poudre*,
named "hidden powder" by fur
trappers for John Jacob Astor.
In 1836, Antoine Janis ordered trappers
to dig a huge cellar along the river
and bury supplies and gun powder.

Today's powder falls upon slopes,
and ski lodge and resort owners
cash-in.

Shoreline Brunch at Galilee

There he is—frying fish again
for those men who left
to follow him around town.
Their feet smelling of myrrh,
they shuffled back here
last week. They haven't
netted a thing since.

I wonder where he got
that catch. He's sizzling
pounds of tilapia,
from our sea, I'll bet ya.
I asked my man if he
had a hand in it,
but he shook his head.

Look now—that's his crew
swerving toward shore.
They're tugging a hundred
pounds or more. Inside nets,
fish flop and tremble—
their eyes glazed like
the men mooring in.

Break on Through—

after "Forest," the painting by Äsa Antalffy Eriksson

A feather falls onto my pillow.
It brings fantasies of woods
with green, dew-matted grass
softer than bunting on my bed.

Sunlight filters through leaves
and outlines trees while I float
in mists hemming the horizon.
I walk on the wind and pretend.

Suddenly, like Alice, I stumble
and fall through dead grass
and dry leaves, then spin counter-
clockwise down a rabbit-hole.

Squirrels skitter across the roof,
and light seeps through vertical blinds,
glimmering with a burst of deception
that this beauty won't end soon.

Dogwood Legend

Two long, two short petals,
the blossoms form a cross
like the one holding Christ
at Golgotha. A legend says
His cross came from a dogwood,
a taller tree 2,000 years ago.
It grew tall as an oak but when cut
for Christ's cross, the dogwood cried.
After nailed upon it, Jesus heard it
weep and decreed future dogwoods
would be lean, bent, and twisted,
too small for any cross.

I pick a blossom and spot,
at its center, blood stains
that might have dripped
from thorns sticking skin.
A red drop falls onto one
of my thighs.

Iphis* Sings New Messages in My Shower

Again, I hear singing above steam,
sizzling new words, streaming
from Iphis, but this time,
in a lilting melody.

"I am Iphis, Jephthah's daughter,"**
it repeats. "I've come to share
the truth of my misery.
I am Jephthah's sole issue—
dead now from society—
locked away a virgin.
No one carries on
our royal dynasty.
So I grieve.
Each year, my friends
visit me in my
self-imposed exile
in these mountains
far from humanity.

Yet here, I play
my tambourine freely,
sing of the Sea of Galilee,
and of the winds
following me
to its quiet shore."

*See George Buchanan's play, *Jephthes*, and Handal's oratorio, *Jephtha*.
**See also *Judges 11: 30-40*.

ACKNOWLEDGMENTS

Many thanks to Brian Daldorph, Silvia Kofler, Gary Lechliter, Jan Duncan O'Neill, Greg Field, Maryfrances Wagner, Carl Bettis, Nancy Eldridge, Pat Lawson, Phil Miller, Kevin Rabas, Robert Stewart, Amy Sage Webb, John Mark Eberhart, Carl Rhoden, Robert Haynes, and Denise Low.

Thank you, Penny Dunning at Chatter House Press, for publishing *Inside Virgil's Garage* in 2013. "Backyard Burial" and "Spring River Swimmers" ran in that collection. And many thanks to j.d.tulloch and 39 West Press.

Thanks to James Benger for creating the 365 Poems in 365 Days group on Facebook. I had already compiled half of these poems, but participating on that site helped me complete the book. Thanks to poets there who regularly encouraged me, including Roy Beckemeyer, Denise Low-Weso, Dan Pohl, Ronda Miller, Melissa Fite Johnson, Diane Wahto, Tyler Shelden, Eve Ott, Beth Gruver Gulley, Nancy Krieg and others who clicked "like."

Special thanks to the kind editors who ran my poems in the following literary magazines, newspapers, and anthologies:

"Backyard Burial," *New Letters* (Vol. 75/4 Fall 2009).
"Since You Left," *Coal City Review* (2014).
"Racing the Rain Home," *I-70 Review* (2014).
"When Hat Dated a Beret" ("Hat Dates a Beret"), *I-70 Review* (2013).
"Hood Ornament," *Thorny Locust* (Vol . 20.2, 2014).
"Diamonds in the Sidewalk," *The Same* (2015).
"Whiteout," *The Kansas City Star*, "Poets Corner" (February 18, 2007).
"Periwinkle Park," *Kansas City Voices* (November 2005),
    also in *Standing on the Edge of the World* (Woodley Press 2008).
"To Phil Miller," *Thorny Locust* (Vol. 18.1, 2011).
"Your Last Christmas," *The Kansas City Star*, "Poets Corner,"
    (December 18, 2005).

"Your Last Two Days," *Coal City Review* (2016).
"My Bones are Glass," *I-70 Review* (2015).
"Messages from My Shower" (Jephthah's Daughter),
    Prompts! A Spontaneous Anthology (39 West Press 2016).
"Re-reading 'The Second Coming' by W.B. Yeats," *The Enigmatist* (2017).
"Economics," *Thorny Locust* (Vol. 20.1, 2013).
"Oliver Twisted," *Tittynope Zine* (Issue 2 2017).
"Frazzled," *Tittynope Zine* (Issue 1 2016).
"Fox Soup," *The Same* (2017).
"Silent Canopy," *Phantom Drift* (2017).
"Whirling Dervishes," *Tittynope Zine* (Issue 2 2017).
"To Catch Leviathan," *Tittynope Zine* (Issue I 2016).
"The Land of Sky Blue Waters," *Thorny Locust* (Vol. 19.2, 2013).
"KC Sky Stations," *Thorny Locust* (Vol. 21.2, 2015).
"Two Mothers with Kids in Winchell's," *Second Touch*
    (Paladin Contemporaries 1992).
"Eyes of Spring," *Thorny Locust* (Vol. 20.1, 2013).
"Vegetable Linguistics," Honorable Mention, Non-Rhyming Poetry,
    85th Annual Writers Digest Contest (2016). *I-70 Review* (2017).
"Poets Make Strange Pets," *Thorny Locust* (Vol 19.2, 2013).
"Mushroom Park," *Flint Hills Review* (Issue 18 2013).
"Spring River Swimmers," *Little Balkans Review* (2010).
"Stuck with a Deck," *I-70 Review* (2016).
"'Brown Sugar' in the Suburbs," *Flint Hills Review* (Issue 21 2016).
"Sturgeon Moon," *56 Days Anthology* (2017).

Lindsey Martin-Bowen is a poet, fiction writer, and educator. She received both her M.A. in English and J.D. from the University of Missouri-Kansas City, where she also taught for eighteen years. Her poems have appeared in *New Letters, I-70 Review, Thorny Locust, Tittynope Zine, Coal City Review, Amethyst Arsenic, Silver Birch Press, Flint Hills Review, Bare Root Review, The Same, Rockhurst Review, Kansas City Voices, Lip Service, Black Bear Review,* and *Phantom Drift.*

A chapbook version of *Crossing Kansas with Jim Morrison,* her third collection of poetry, was a semi-finalist in a 2015-16 QuillsEdge Press contest. Her preceding collection, *Inside Virgil's Garage,* was a runner-up for the 2015 Nelson Poetry Book Award, and a poem from that volume was nominated for a Pushcart Prize. Last year, in its 85th annual contest, *Writer's Digest* awarded her "Vegetable Linguistics" an Honorable Mention, and in 2008, McClatchy Newspapers named her debut collection, *Standing on the Edge of the World,* one of the Ten Top poetry books of the year.

Martin-Bowen has worked as a reporter for *The Louisville Times* and *The SUN Newspapers,* as an associate editor for *Modern Jeweler Magazine,* and as editor of *The National Paralegal Reporter.* She currently teaches writing at MCC-Longview.

CPSIA information can be obtained
at www.ICGtesting.com
Printed in the USA
FFOW02n0625230717
38003FF